WONDERFUL
WATER EXPERIMENTS FOR ELEMENTARY STUDENTS

SCIENCE BOOK FOR KIDS 9-12
CHILDREN'S SCIENCE EDUCATION BOOKS

BABY PROFESSOR
EDUCATION KIDS

In this book, we're going to talk about some fun experiments with water. So, let's get right to it!

Do you remember the first time you put a toy boat in your bathtub and it floated? Water has lots of interesting properties that you can explore by setting up some experiments at home or in school. You should always have an adult help you when you're doing experiments. Safety first!

EXPERIMENT 1:
THE FLOATING PAPERCLIP

This experiment demonstrates the surface tension of water.

THINGS YOU'LL NEED:

You'll need some clean paper clips that are dry. You'll need a glass bowl of water. You'll also need some tissue paper about one half the size of a dollar bill and a pencil with an eraser. The type of tissue you should use is like lightweight wrapping paper.

WHAT TO DO:

Step 1: Pour some water into the bowl.

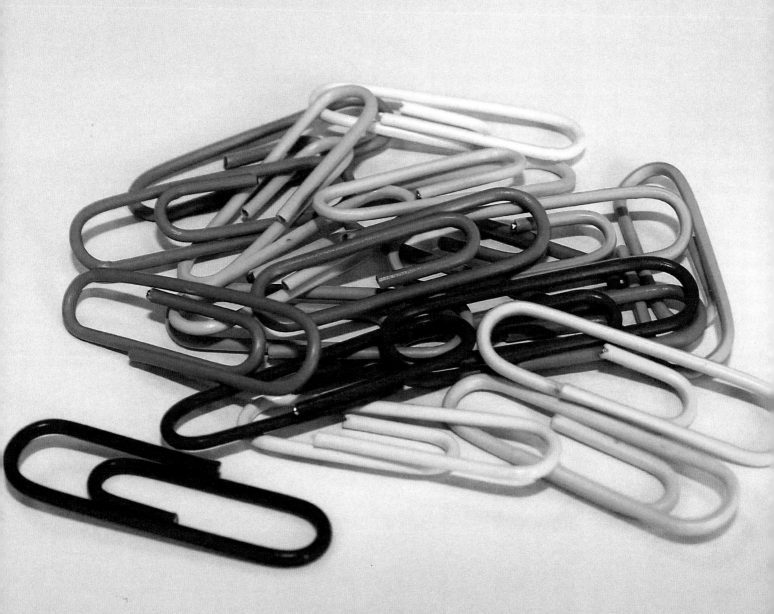

Step 4: Now put a clean, dry paper clip gently on the surface of the tissue. Make sure you don't tap the water or the paper when you're doing this part!

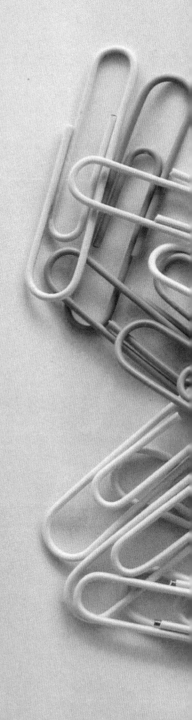

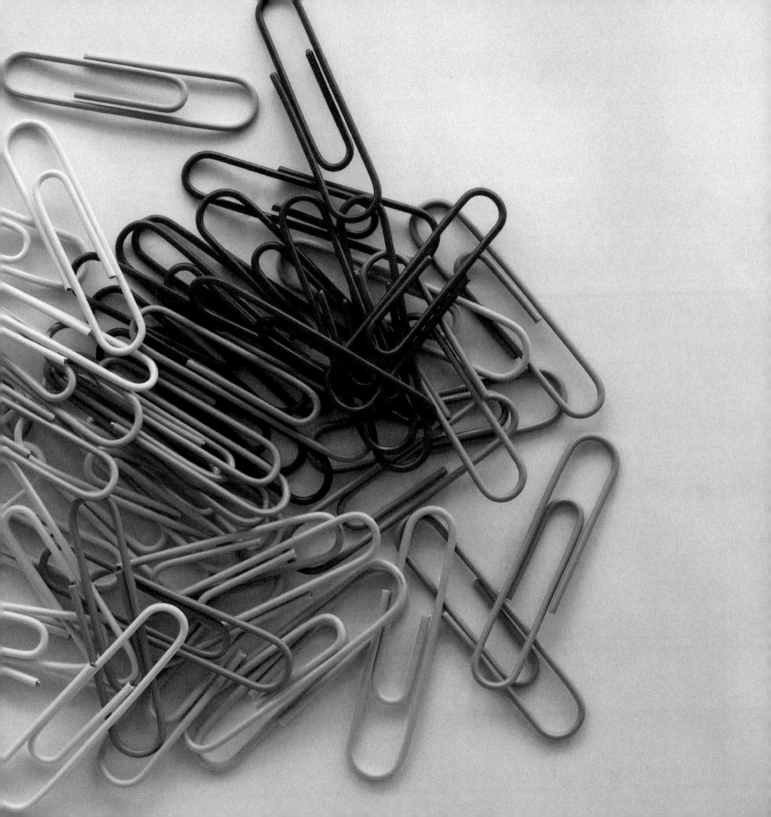

Step 5: Using the eraser end of your pencil, try poking the tissue paper without hitting the paper clip until the paper sinks. If you're careful, the tissue paper will sink, but the paper clip will be left floating on the surface!

THE SCIENCE BEHIND IT:

When you first placed the paper clip on the surface of the water it sank, so why is it floating now? It has to do with the surface tension of the water. On the water's surface, the molecules of water are holding each other tightly. When the conditions are just right, they can be holding each other in unison with a strong enough bond to support the weight of the paperclip. Even though it looks like it's floating, it's really being held in place by the water's surface tension. Water striders are one of the types of insects that use this surface tension of water to walk along a stream's surface.

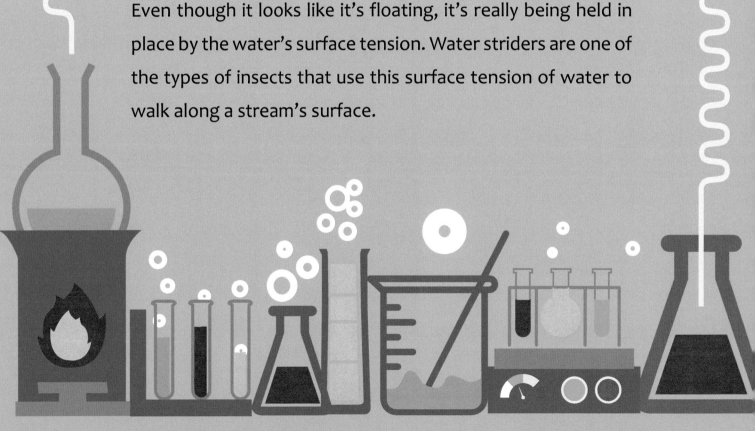

EXPERIMENT 2:
INSTANT "LAVA"

This experiment demonstrates the difference in density between oil and water.

THINGS YOU'LL NEED:

You'll need a transparent drinking glass. You'll need about ¼ cup of oil, the vegetable type. You'll need a teaspoon of salt and some water. You'll need some food coloring, whichever color you like.

WHAT TO DO:

Step 1: Pour water into the glass so it's about three-fourths full.

Step 2: Put in about 5 droplets of food dye, whichever color you like.

Step 3: Pour the oil slowly into the glass. At this point, because oil and water don't mix, the oil will float over the water. This is an interesting effect, but it gets better!

Step 4: Sprinkle the salt on the top of the oil's surface.

Step 5: Observe as your "lava" globs go up and then down inside the glass!

Step 6: You can keep the "lava" going by adding another teaspoon of salt.

THE SCIENCE BEHIND IT:

Of course, this isn't real "lava," but it produces an effect like an old-fashioned lava lamp. When you pour the oil in, it settles at the water's surface because it is less dense than water. However, the granules of salt are heavier than the vegetable oil so they sink down and take some oil along for the ride. When the salt granules dissolve, the oil doesn't have anything to weigh it down, so it bounces back up again.

EXPERIMENT 3:
"PAINT" A CARNATION

This experiment demonstrates the process of transpiration in plants.

THINGS YOU'LL NEED:

You'll need some white carnations from your local florist. You'll also need some food coloring, some water, and some tall glasses.

WHAT TO DO:

Step 1: Decide what colors you would like to use for your flowers.

Step 2: Fill the glasses three-fourths full with cold, tap water.

Step 3: Place enough droplets of food coloring in each glass so you can see the color, just as if you were coloring eggs. If you don't make the color dark enough you won't be able to see it as distinctly once the flower absorbs it.

Step 4: Cut off the last inch or so of each carnation stem and place one carnation in each glass. You can try a different color for each carnation.

Step 5: You'll have to be patient to see the results of your experiment. It might just take a few hours or it might take 1-2 days.

Step 6: Eventually, you'll see the carnations become different colors.

Step 7: If you want to try it, get an adult to use a razor blade to cut the flower's stem about 3-4 inches. Then, you can place each different part of the stem in different colors to create a two-color flower!

THE SCIENCE BEHIND IT:

This experiment shows the process of transpiration. The plant brings water up vertically into the stem. The water then evaporates through the flower petals and leaves through special openings called stomata. As the water goes through the process of evaporating, it forms pressure in the stem that brings even more water up, the same way you bring liquid into a straw. Some trees and larger plants can transpire water in the amount of hundreds of gallons when the temperature is hot outdoors. Try some different environmental changes, like a dark room and a sunny room, to see which carnations transpire the most. You'll be able to tell because the flower with the most color will have transpired the most.

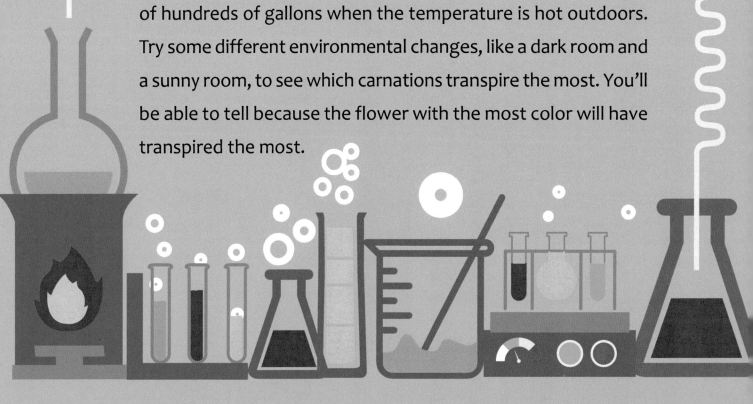

EXPERIMENT 4:
THE CARTESIAN DIVER

This experiment is based on a classic experiment that shows the density of water versus air.

THINGS YOU'LL NEED:

You'll need a clear one-liter plastic bottle with its cap. Don't use a 2-liter bottle. It's too big. You'll also need the pen cap from a ballpoint pen and enough water to fill up the bottle. Make sure the cap from the ballpoint pen doesn't have any holes in it. The last thing you'll need is a small piece of modeling clay.

WHAT TO DO:

Step 1: Make sure to remove any of the labels that are wrapped around your bottle so you can witness what's going on in the inside.

Step 2: Completely fill up the bottle with tap water.

Step 3: Wrap a tiny pea-sized piece of modeling clay around the end of the pen cap.

Step 4: Place the end of the pen cap into the bottle so that the modeling clay goes in first. A small amount of water will spill out. That's okay. The pen cap should be just barely floating. If it's sinking instead, take it out and reduce the amount of clay. If it's floating too much, you'll need to place some additional clay on the end of the cap.

Step 5: Once you get it just right, put the bottle cap back on and make sure it's screwed on tight.

Step 6. Now you can make your "diver" go up and down by squeezing the bottle. If you squeeze if forcefully, the "diver" will go down. When you stop holding tight, the "diver" travels to the surface. With some practice, you can get your "diver" to stop at the bottle's center.

Step 7: If your "diver" isn't cooperating, fool around some more with the amount of clay and make sure that the bottle is completely filled with water before you replace the cap.

Step 8: Instead of the pen cap, you can make a soy sauce diver. Those small packets of soy sauce that come with Chinese food will work the same way as your pen cap because they have a bubble of air inside them.

THE SCIENCE BEHIND IT:

This experiment comes from the famous mathematician and scientist René Descartes. That's why it's called a "Cartesian" diver. This experiment is a demonstration of density. As you hold the bottle tightly, the bubble of air inside the pen's cap gets smaller or compresses down. That makes the pen cap denser than the water it's suspended in, making it sink. When you stop holding tightly, the bubble of air increases in size again and that makes your "diver" rise again, since water is forced out of the pen cap thrusting it upwards.

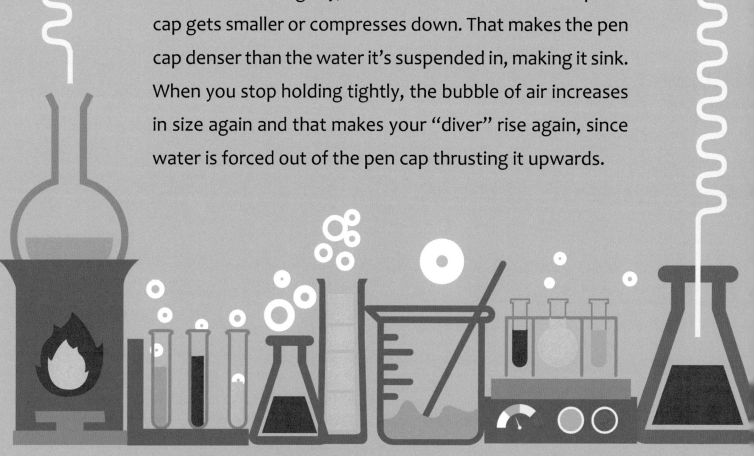

RENE DESCARTES

WATER EXPERIMENTS ARE FUN!

Make sure you work with an adult whenever you perform experiments at home or at school. Before you set up the experiment, form a hypothesis about what you think will happen when you conduct the experiment. Write it down in your science journal. Then, after you've conducted the experiment, write down your results. Was your hypothesis correct or not? By coming up with a hypothesis and performing your experiment to test it, you're using the scientific method. You can also alter the experiment to see if you get different results.

Awesome! Now that you've finished these fun water experiments, you may want to perform some experiments that explode in the Baby Professor book Exploding Experiments for Exceptional Learners – Science Book for Kids 9-12.

Visit

BABY PROFESSOR
EDUCATION KIDS

www.BabyProfessorBooks.com

to download Free Baby Professor eBooks
and view our catalog of new and exciting
Children's Books

Made in the USA
Monee, IL
19 November 2020